This Book Belongs to:

Instrument:

Copyright   2022

All rights reserved
No parts of the publication may be reproduced, distributed, or transmitted in any form or by any means including photocopying, recording, or other electronic or mechanical methods without prior written permission from the publisher.

How to use this book:

This book will help you with your daily practice. You or your teacher can write in it what you need to do each week and what your goal is. You can keep track of how many times you've managed to practise by colouring in or ticking the stars. There are some helpful practice tips too.

Practising performing is really important so give a performance each week, even if it's only to the cat! It can even be just a few lines of a piece you're learning. Walk on stage, bow, announce what you're going to play and don't forget to bow at the end!

Have fun and enjoy your music making!

⭐ Create an area in the house where you can practise undisturbed and focus easily.

Date: 10/01/21

Goal for the week: To learn my concerto off by heart

Technical points to remember:
Keep my fingers soft on the bow and my thumb curved

Notes:

Practise G major scale and arpeggio two octaves to warm up.

Practise the pieces on page 26 and do all the dynamics.

Practise the Mozart piece with a metronome.

Listen to my new piece on Youtube.

This week I performed

_____Allegro_____ to _____My class_____

Date:

Goal for the week:

Technical points to remember:

Notes:

This week I performed

_____to_____

_____
_____
_____
_____
_____

_____
_____
_____
_____
_____

☆ ☆ ☆ ☆ ☆ ☆ ☆

Date:

Goal for the week:

Technical points to remember:

Notes:

This week I performed

_____to_____

_____
_____
_____
_____
_____

_____
_____
_____
_____

☆ ☆ ☆ ☆ ☆ ☆ ☆

Date:

Goal for the week:

Technical points to remember:

Notes:

This week I performed

_____to_____

_____
_____
_____
_____
_____

_____
_____
_____
_____
_____

☆ ☆ ☆ ☆ ☆ ☆ ☆

⭐ Practise as regularly as possible – little and often is better than a long session less often.

Date:

Goal for the week:

Technical points to remember:

Notes:

This week I performed

_____to_____

☆ ☆ ☆ ☆ ☆ ☆ ☆

Date:

Goal for the week:

Technical points to remember:

Notes:

This week I performed

_____to_____

☆ ☆ ☆ ☆ ☆ ☆ ☆

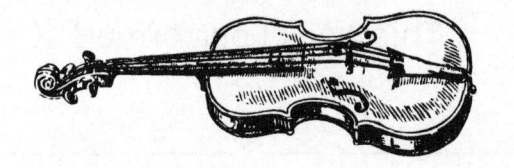

"Practice puts brains in your muscles."

Sam Snead

Date:

Goal for the week:

Technical points to remember:

Notes:

This week I performed

_____to_____

_____
_____
_____
_____
_____

_____
_____
_____
_____
_____

☆ ☆ ☆ ☆ ☆ ☆ ☆

Date:

Goal for the week:

Technical points to remember:

Notes:

This week I performed

_____to_____

_____
_____
_____
_____
_____
_____

_____
_____
_____
_____
_____
_____

☆ ☆ ☆ ☆ ☆ ☆ ☆ ☆

⭐ Pick out the notes or bars that are troublesome – fix them then REPEAT. Then take a run up from a couple of bars before.

Date:

Goal for the week:

Technical points to remember:

Notes:

This week I performed

_____to_____

_____
_____
_____
_____
_____
_____

_____
_____
_____
_____
_____

☆ ☆ ☆ ☆ ☆ ☆ ☆

Date:

Goal for the week:

Technical points to remember:

Notes:

This week I performed

_____ to _____

_____
_____
_____
_____
_____

_____
_____
_____
_____
_____

☆ ☆ ☆ ☆ ☆ ☆ ☆

"Music, a magic far beyond all we do here."

J.K. Rowling

Date:

Goal for the week:

Technical points to remember:

Notes:

This week I performed

_____to_____

―――――――――――――――――――――――――
―――――――――――――――――――――――――
―――――――――――――――――――――――――
―――――――――――――――――――――――――
―――――――――――――――――――――――――

―――――――――――――――――――――――――
―――――――――――――――――――――――――
―――――――――――――――――――――――――
―――――――――――――――――――――――――
―――――――――――――――――――――――――

☆ ☆ ☆ ☆ ☆ ☆ ☆

Date:

Goal for the week:

Technical points to remember:

Notes:

This week I performed

_____to_____

_____
_____
_____
_____
_____

_____
_____
_____
_____
_____

☆ ☆ ☆ ☆ ☆ ☆ ☆

⭐ Notice any words in your piece that tell you about the character or speed of what you are playing.

Date:

Goal for the week:

Technical points to remember:

Notes:

This week I performed

_____ to _____

_____
_____
_____
_____
_____

_____
_____
_____
_____
_____

☆ ☆ ☆ ☆ ☆ ☆ ☆

Date:

Goal for the week:

Technical points to remember:

Notes:

This week I performed

_____to_____

_____
_____
_____
_____
_____

_____
_____
_____
_____
_____

☆ ☆ ☆ ☆ ☆ ☆ ☆

Date:

Goal for the week:

Technical points to remember:

Notes:

This week I performed

_____to_____

_____
_____
_____
_____
_____
_____

_____
_____
_____
_____
_____

☆ ☆ ☆ ☆ ☆ ☆ ☆

"Knowledge is a treasure but practice is the key."

Lao Tzu

Date:

Goal for the week:

Technical points to remember:

Notes:

This week I performed

_____to_____

_____
_____
_____
_____
_____

_____
_____
_____
_____

☆ ☆ ☆ ☆ ☆ ☆ ☆

⭐ Practise difficult bars in slow-motion then gradually make them faster. You'll learn them quicker this way.

Date:

Goal for the week:

Technical points to remember:

Notes:

This week I performed

_____to_____

☆ ☆ ☆ ☆ ☆ ☆ ☆

Date:

Goal for the week:

Technical points to remember:

Notes:

This week I performed

_____to_____

_____
_____
_____
_____
_____
_____

_____
_____
_____
_____
_____

☆ ☆ ☆ ☆ ☆ ☆ ☆

Date:

Goal for the week:

Technical points to remember:

Notes:

This week I performed

_____to_____

_____
_____
_____
_____
_____
_____

_____
_____
_____
_____
_____
_____

☆ ☆ ☆ ☆ ☆ ☆ ☆

"You can't download a live musical experience."

House of Blues

Date:

Goal for the week:

Technical points to remember:

Notes:

This week I performed

_____to_____

_____
_____
_____
_____
_____
_____

_____
_____
_____
_____
_____

☆ ☆ ☆ ☆ ☆ ☆ ☆

⭐ If you have a fast passage with lots of notes and you find it hard, try playing each note twice. Then play without repeated notes but with the left hand only (without the bow.) Now try it as written again.

Date:

Goal for the week:

Technical points to remember:

Notes:

This week I performed

_____to_____

_____
_____
_____
_____
_____

_____
_____
_____
_____
_____

☆ ☆ ☆ ☆ ☆ ☆ ☆

Date:

Goal for the week:

Technical points to remember:

Notes:

This week I performed

_____to_____

_____
_____
_____
_____
_____
_____

_____
_____
_____
_____
_____
_____

☆ ☆ ☆ ☆ ☆ ☆ ☆

Date:

Goal for the week:

Technical points to remember:

Notes:

This week I performed

_____to_____

_____
_____
_____
_____
_____

_____
_____
_____
_____
_____

☆ ☆ ☆ ☆ ☆ ☆

"Music is the heart of life."

Franz Liszt

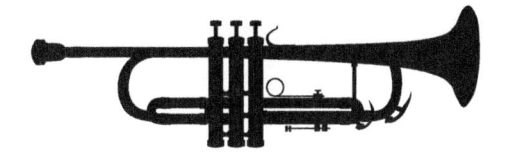

Date:

Goal for the week:

Technical points to remember:

Notes:

This week I performed

_____to_____

_____
_____
_____
_____
_____

_____
_____
_____
_____
_____

☆ ☆ ☆ ☆ ☆ ☆ ☆

⭐ Try playing your piece with a metronome. Can you stay in time with it?

Date:

Goal for the week:

Technical points to remember:

Notes:

This week I performed

_____ to _____

_____
_____
_____
_____
_____
_____

_____
_____
_____
_____
_____
_____

☆ ☆ ☆ ☆ ☆ ☆ ☆

Date:

Goal for the week:

Technical points to remember:

Notes:

This week I performed

_____ to _____

_____
_____
_____
_____
_____

_____
_____
_____
_____

☆ ☆ ☆ ☆ ☆ ☆ ☆

Date:

Goal for the week:

Technical points to remember:

Notes:

This week I performed

_____ to _____

_____
_____
_____
_____
_____

_____
_____
_____
_____
_____

☆ ☆ ☆ ☆ ☆ ☆ ☆

"Without music, life would be a mistake."

Friedrich Nietzsche

Date:

Goal for the week:

Technical points to remember:

Notes:

This week I performed

_____to_____

_____
_____
_____
_____
_____

_____
_____
_____
_____
_____

☆ ☆ ☆ ☆ ☆ ☆ ☆

⭐ Does the piece you're playing sound like one person telling a story or is there more than one character? What are they like—angry, sad, joyful or dreamy?

Date:

Goal for the week:

Technical points to remember:

Notes:

This week I performed

_____to_____

_____
_____
_____
_____
_____

_____
_____
_____
_____
_____

☆ ☆ ☆ ☆ ☆ ☆ ☆

Date:

Goal for the week:

Technical points to remember:

Notes:

This week I performed

_____to_____

_____
_____
_____
_____
_____
_____

_____
_____
_____
_____
_____

☆ ☆ ☆ ☆ ☆ ☆ ☆

Date:

Goal for the week:

Technical points to remember:

Notes:

This week I performed

_____to_____

_____
_____
_____
_____
_____
_____

_____
_____
_____
_____
_____

☆ ☆ ☆ ☆ ☆ ☆ ☆

Date:

Goal for the week:

Technical points to remember:

Notes:

This week I performed

_____to_____

_____
_____
_____
_____
_____
_____

_____
_____
_____
_____
_____

☆ ☆ ☆ ☆ ☆ ☆ ☆

Date:

Goal for the week:

Technical points to remember:

Notes:

This week I performed

_____to_____

_____
_____
_____
_____
_____

_____
_____
_____
_____
_____

☆ ☆ ☆ ☆ ☆ ☆ ☆

Date:

Goal for the week:

Technical points to remember:

Notes:

This week I performed

_____to_____

☆ ☆ ☆ ☆ ☆ ☆ ☆

Date:

Goal for the week:

Technical points to remember:

Notes:

This week I performed

_____to_____

_____
_____
_____
_____
_____
_____

_____
_____
_____
_____
_____
_____

☆ ☆ ☆ ☆ ☆ ☆ ☆

⭐ When performing, don't try to 'relax' but enjoy the extra excited energy you feel, it will help your performance!

Date:

Goal for the week:

Technical points to remember:

Notes:

This week I performed

_____to_____

_____
_____
_____
_____
_____

_____
_____
_____
_____
_____

☆ ☆ ☆ ☆ ☆ ☆ ☆

Notes:

Printed in Great Britain
by Amazon